This Book Belongs To ___Julia & Victoria Garrick___

*Dedicated to the memory of P. J. Becker.
He fought valiantly his entire life and had the heart
of a champion. We will miss you, but never forget your
zest for life. May God be with you and your family.*

GEORGE AND ROBERT

CATHOLIC EDITION

BIBLE
BLESSINGS

Written by Alice Joyce Davidson
Illustrated by Victoria Marshall

Regina Press New York

Alice went to Bible School
To learn of God's great ways.

She read the Psalms and Proverbs
For advice and words of praise.

Alice thought of all she learned
And knew it would be fun

To make up rhymes and songs of praise
To share with everyone.

Joy comes with the morning.

Psalm 30.5

The sun is smiling at me.
Joy is in the air!
A brand new day has started.
God's love is everywhere.

This is the day that the Lord has made;
let us rejoice and be glad in it.

Psalm 118:24

Every second,
    every minute,
Every day
    has glad things in it.
For every day
    the whole year through
Was made by God
    for me and you.

I praise you,
for I am fearfully and wonderfully made.

Psalm 139:14

God made me and I can talk,
And I can sing, and pray;
I can touch, and smell, and hear,
And see new joys each day;
For God gave me a mind, and heart—
A soul that knows His way.

So teach us to count our days
that we may gain a wise heart.

Psalm 90:12

There's so much, God,
   to see, to hear,
There's so much, God, to know,
Please stay beside me
   day by day
And help me learn and grow!

A desire realized is sweet to the soul.
Psalm 13:19

How nice it is to have a dream—
A special goal to do.
How sweet it is when goals are met
And happy dreams come true!

Know well the condition of your flocks.

Proverbs 27:23

Kitty cats to cuddle,
Puppy dogs to run—
Having pets to care for
Is a special kind of fun!

Whoever walks with the wise, becomes wise.

Proverbs 13:20

Pick somebody wiser
Whom you can walk beside
And you'll see a whole lot better
As your eyes will open wide.
Pick somebody wiser
Whom you can listen to
And you'll be a whole lot smarter
In everything you do.

Even children make themselves known by their acts,
by whether what they do is pure and right.

Proverbs 20:11

I've got a lot to learn yet,
    but I know one thing for sure—
I feel good when I do my best
    and when my heart is pure.

Commit your work to the Lord,
and your plans will be established.

Proverbs 16:3

If what you do is for the Lord,
Then you will have a sweet reward . . .
For all who follow in His way
Are blessed with peace and joy each day.

Create in me a clean heart, O God,
and put a new and right spirit within me.

Psalm 51:10

Please help me, God, be better,
I'd like that if You would,
Because I know You're happier
When I'm especially good.

You made summer and winter.

Psalm 74:17

Summer, winter, spring and fall
Are filled with wonders through and through;
For every season, one and all,
Was made by God who made us, too.

Blessed be the Lord, who daily
bears us up.

Psalm 68:19

In front of me,
    behind me,
        above me, and around me,
Everywhere I go,
    I know
        God's loving gifts surround me!

Trust in the Lord with all your heart,
and do not rely on your own insight.

Proverbs 3:5

Sometimes it's hard to understand
Why this or that is so,
But trust the Lord—He'll answer
When the time is right to know.

O Lord, attend to my cry:
give ear to my prayer.

Psalm 17:1

When I'm feeling troubled
And my heart is filled with care,
I gather up my troubles
And go to God in prayer.
And when I'm feeling good again
And joy is everywhere,
I pay God a little visit
With a happy thank-you prayer.

The human mind plans the way,
but the Lord directs the steps.

Proverbs 16:9

I can go from there to here,
Or go from here to there,
And everywhere I go, God IS—
For God is everywhere!

I fear no evil;
for you are with me.

Psalm 23:4

When I'm afraid, I close my eyes
And say a prayer . . . and then
I feel God watching over me
And I'm okay again!

Do not enter the path of the wicked,
and do not walk in the way of evildoers.

Proverbs 4:14

There's a two-letter word
That's easily heard
When temptation comes your way . . .

If you think you may stray
Just remember to say
That two-letter word—
NO!

The Lord is gracious and merciful,
slow to anger and abounding in steadfast love.

Psalm 145:8

Sometimes when I'm bad,
It makes me quite sad,
But I know that the good Lord above
Forgives what I do,
and blesses me, too,
With His special and wonderful love!

A soft answer turns away wrath.

Proverbs 15:1

When someone talks with anger,
Don't let it get you down . . .
Answer anger with a smile
And you'll chase away a frown!

Pleasant words are like a honeycomb,
sweetness to the soul
and health to the body.

Proverbs 16:24

Give someone an extra lift
With pleasant words of praise
For compliments are special gifts
That add such joy to days.

A glad heart makes a cheerful countenance.

Proverbs 15:13

A great big smile
Is so worthwhile,
It brightens up a day
For sad folks, mad folks,
Already glad folks—
And all who come your way!

What is desirable in a person is loyalty.

Proverbs 19:22

Caring, sharing, being kind—
That's what life's about . . .
God fills our hearts with lots of love
Which we, in turn, give out.

How very good and pleasant it is
when kindred live together in unity!

Psalm 133:1

I've small friends, tall friends,
light friends, dark friends,
friends of every kind . . .
And everywhere I go
I know new friends
are nice to find!

A friend loves at all times.

Proverbs 17:17

Who's with me
When I'm up or down?
Who cheers me
When I wear a frown?
Who has a helping hand
To lend?
MY FRIEND!

A true friend sticks closer
than one's nearest kin.

Proverbs 18:24

Lend a hand, and give an ear,
Share a dream or plan—
To have a friend, just be a friend
In every way you can.

Those who counsel peace have joy.

Proverbs 12:20

Let's join our hands and work for good,
And work for peace and brotherhood;
Let's understand each other's ways
And help bring peaceful, happy days.

It is good
to give thanks to the Lord.

Psalm 92:1

Thank You, God, for loving parents,
Thank You, God, for food to eat.
Thank You, God, for all Your seasons,
For winter's snow, for summer's heat.
Thank You, God, for glowing rainbows,
Thank You, God, for birds that sing.
Thank You, God, for all Your wonders,
Thank You, God, for everything!

Worship the Lord with gladness;
come into his presence with singing.

Psalm 100:2

I have a song of thanks to sing
For all the happy things You bring,
Thank You, Lord, for everything.
I thank You, Lord, Amen!

I feel a song of praise is due
For all the gifts we get from You,
For all the love You give us, too,
I love You, Lord, Amen!

The Lord is my shepherd, I shall not want.

Psalm 23:1

He is my shepherd,
I am His lamb,
The closer to God,
the happier I am!